Are The Unevangelized Really Lost?

Dr. Carl J. Broggi

ISBN:1539749215
ISBN-13:9781539749219

DEDICATION

TO AUDREY

WHOSE VERY LIFE IS GOOD NEWS SHARED

CONTENTS

OBJECTIVES

As a result of this study of this topic we want to be able to:

- Demonstrate the complexity of this question
  to other realms of theology.

- Define the biblical claim concerning salvation through Christ
  alone.

- Understand the non-biblical responses to the biblical claim.

- Examine the general revelation God has given
  of Himself to all people.

- Discover the relationship between general revelation
  and specific revelation.

- Consider our responsibility in light of the fate of the
  unevangelized.

- Memorize John 14:6 and Acts 4:12.

I. UNDERSTANDING THE COMPLEXITY
OF THE QUESTION

Framing The Question

The approximate population of the world is now approaching 8 billion people. A billion is a challenging number to get our mind around but can become an understandable value when we apply it to time. One billion days ago the world was not yet created. One billion hours ago the Book of Genesis had not yet been written. One billion minutes ago Jesus Christ was still on the earth. One billion seconds ago World War II was still unfolding. To put it in monetary terms, our government is spending 10.460 billion per day (of which 4.506 billion is borrowed). It is essential that we as born-again believers picture the billions of people on planet earth not simply as a mass of humanity but as individuals for whom Christ died and God loves. The Lord taught that a person's soul was of eternal worth.

"For what does it profit a man to gain the whole world, and forfeit his soul? "For what will a man give in exchange for his soul?"
(Mark 8:36-37)

When a Christian looks at the unevangelized billions they must conceive them on a stage covering every nation on the planet and in a time frame that will last for all of eternity.

Carl J. Broggi

"These will go away into eternal punishment, but the righteous into eternal life." (Matthew 25:46)

Of the approximate 7.7 billion people on the earth, about one-third are nominally Christian (the true Christians are obviously much less according to Christ in Matthew 7:13-14), about one third are uninterested in Christianity, and about one third have never heard the name of Jesus Christ. With over half of the world living in spiritual darkness the Christian must sincerely ask, "Are the untold billions really lost and headed to hell?" According to the U.S. Center for World Missions, ninety percent of all missionaries work among people who have some exposure to Christianity while only about ten percent serve among people who have never even heard the name of Christ. Part of the problem concerning Christian people taking the gospel to the neglected masses is rooted in a theological question, namely, are these people who have never even heard of Jesus' name really lost?

The Controversy Behind The Question

This is certainly a common objection that non-Christians use as an excuse not to believe and receive Christ as their Savior. Sometimes unbelievers have objections they place before Christians not because they want an answer—but because they want to put before us a "smokescreen" so they can justify their unbelief. Sometimes people have objections because Satan is trying to give them a reason not to believe (Ephesians 6:12). Sometimes people have objections because they are asking an honest question from a searching heart (Mark 12:28-34). Whatever their motive, the rationale behind their question is that God must be both unjust and unloving to send the unevangelized to hell. The essence of their question is, "How can Christianity teach God is loving and just if He sends people to hell because they have not trusted in Jesus of whom they have never heard?"

The Questions Behind The Question

The question concerning the state of the unevangelized may on the surface appear to be an innocent question for theologians and college

2

students and others who like to engage in stimulating dialogue. In reality, the question, "Are the heathen really lost?" is an issue that not only the intellectual skeptic must answer, but the sincere Christian who should be the most concerned about the state of the unevangelized. This question is really a profound question because behind this seemingly harmless question are other questions about theology. The character of God is questioned, "Is God really just and fair?", which is a challenge to the doctrine of God (Pateriology). The necessity of Golgotha is questioned, "Did Christ really have to die?", which is a challenge to the doctrine of salvation (Soteriology). The uniqueness of Christ is questioned, "Is Christ really the only way?", which is a challenge to the doctrine of Christ (Christology). The corruption of man is questioned, "Is man evil by nature?", which is a challenge to the doctrine of man (Anthropology). The judgment of God on sin is questioned, "Is sin all that bad?", which is a challenge to the doctrine of sin (Hamartiology). The role of God's people is questioned, "Are God's people a unique witness?", which is a challenge to the doctrine of the church (Ecclesiology). The manner in which God will sum up history is questioned, "Is there a future judgment where people will go to either heaven or hell?", which is a challenge to the doctrine of the church (Ecclesiology). The manner in which God will sum up history is questioned, "Is there a future judgment where people will go to either heaven or hell?", which is a challenge to the doctrine of future things (Eschatology). "Are the heathen really lost?" on the surface appears to be a simple question but it strikes at the very foundations of Christian theology.

II. UNDERSTANDING THE SOLUTION TO THE QUESTION

The Biblical Claim Of Salvation Only Through Christ

There are four premises throughout the Bible that claim salvation is only through Jesus Christ: (1) Jesus claimed to be the only way to God (Jn. 3:18; 6:29; 14:6); (2) Jesus' followers testified that He was the only way to God (Acts 4:12; 10:43; 16:31; Romans 10:9-15; 1 Timothy 2:5); (3) Jesus claimed other ways of salvation are false and unacceptable to God (John 3:18; 8:19, 24, 41-42, 44, 47); (4) Jesus' followers claimed other ways of salvation are false and unacceptable to God (Acts 13:39; 17:17-18; Romans 10:9-15; 1 Corinthians 10:20; 2 Thessalonians 1:8-9). If you base your authority on the Bible the only conclusion you can draw from these four premises is that Jesus is the only way of salvation and all other religions are false.

The False Biblical Claim Of Salvation Via A Second Chance

Some who are unwilling to deny the clear truths of the above passages, attempt to circumvent these truths by saying there is some kind of a second chance after death citing passages like 1 Peter 4:6:

"For the gospel has for this purpose been preached even to those who are dead, that though they are judged in the flesh as men, they may live in the spirit according to the will of God."

If we look carefully at this verse it is evident that the Apostle Peter is referring to believers and not unbelievers. So we must ask, "When was the gospel preached "to those who are dead?" The gospel was preached to the dead when they were alive because clearly the Apostle Peter does not say, "the gospel IS for this purpose BEING preached" but he says, "the gospel HAS for this purpose been preached even to those who are dead." They are 'dead' now, but they were alive when they heard 'the gospel.' This verse is speaking about those who have been martyred. Clearly and contextually, he is not speaking of the lost dead but of the saved dead. In this paragraph of Scripture the Apostle Peter is addressing the persecution of Christians and he is reminding his readers that certain lost men judged believers while they were on earth in the form of persecution in that they put them to death. In order to skirt the fate of the unevangelized, those who attempt to take a more orthodox position by appealing to passages like this miss the context of the verse's teaching. The Bible is very clear that "the gospel" is preached only to the living because there is no chance for salvation after death. Hebrews plainly says, **"And as it is appointed for men to die once, but after this the judgment"** and not a second chance (Hebrews 9:27).

The Non-Biblical Response To The Biblical Claim

Some unbelievers argue for *universalism*. Universalism is the belief that everyone will be saved, advocating that all people eventually end up in heaven. This theology is often driven by the belief that a life of eternal torment in hell is morally reprehensible. Universalism teaches that since God is so full of love and mercy He will never let anyone go to hell (if there is such a place). This belief is a denial of Acts 4:12 and 1 Timothy 2:5.

Others however, argue for *pluralism*. Pluralism claims that there are dimensions of truth in all religions and therefore all religions are of equal value and need to be respected as a path to pursue. And since all religions are of "equal" value there needs to be some level of unity and cooperation (ecumenicism). While there are some similarities in most of the religions of the world – the one true God as revealed in the Bible is unique. Moses rejected any so-called 'revelation' of God found in other religions as a form of idolatry to be rejected (Exodus 20:2-3). Jesus' claim to be the only way to the Father is a mutually exclusive claim making all other claims false (John 3:18, 36, 14:6). Based on the revelation of God in Scripture, we are once again reminded that the only valid answer to the state of the unevangelized is found in the clear teaching of the Bible and not mere speculation.

Finally, some argue for *inclusivism*. Inclusivism argues that while only Christianity is true, God still imputes salvation to any person who is sincere in his belief. Inclusivism teaches that a person can appropriate the benefits of Christ's death and resurrection without actually believing in Him. This view teaches Christ is the only Savior and that Christianity is the only true religion. But it also teaches that this salvation can be appropriated without necessarily believing in Jesus. This view advocates that adherents of other religions and even atheists can be saved by responding to God's general revelation. **This position is contrary to the biblical view of *exclusivism* which teaches that a sinner can only be saved by a conscious, explicit faith in the gospel of Jesus Christ** (John 3:16-18; Ephesians 2:3). The Bible is very clear that there is no middle ground concerning placing one's faith in Jesus Christ (1 John 5:11-13). If the Bible is God's Word – then man's reasoning must yield to God's revelation. To consider Christianity as just another commodity on the world religious market is to deny the clear revelation of God in Scripture.

III. THE BIBLICAL RESPONSE TO THE BIBLICAL CLAIM

All People Everywhere Have Some Light About God

All people, no matter who they are or where they live on this planet, have some light, some knowledge, some revelation about God. In Romans 1, while the Apostle Paul does not use the term 'light,' to describe God's general revelation (Psalm 119:105; 2 Peter 1:19), he does use the opposite term 'darkness' (Romans 1:21) and he uses 'truth' as a synonym for 'light' in Romans 1:18. The Bible teaches that all men have 'light' given through at least two witnesses: the creation around us and the conscience within.

The Bible is clear that all men have the testimony of God as the Creator of the world as seen in the creation around them (Romans 1:18-20). Every leaf, every flower, every drop of water and every person bears the stamp, "Made by God." The creation around us points to the truth that there must be a Creator (Psalm 19:1-4; Acts 14:17).

In addition, the Bible also teaches that God has revealed Himself to all men through the conscience within (Romans 1:18, 32; 2:14-15). Gentile pagans who have no "Bible" still are able to discern between right and wrong because God has written the Law within their hearts. This is why the Apostle Paul makes very clear in Romans 1:18-3:18 that all people have some knowledge of God – be they the hard core pagan, the moral man, or the religious Jew. After he demonstrates this truth, he then confronts each group with the uncomfortable fact that they have not lived up to that knowledge and therefore are inexcusably guilty. His basic premise in the opening chapters of Romans is that no one can plead innocence because no one can plead ignorance. Nonetheless, he also shows us here in Romans 1:18-32 that the just judgment of God on the unevangelized is neither irrational or unfair beginning with this first premise that all people have some light.

When The Light God Gives Is Refused Darkness Increases

If a person refuses the revelation of God given in creation and conscience then he begins to develop false concepts about God (Romans 1:21). In fact, Romans 1:21 is the verse liberal "Christian" theologians use to argue that a man can know God through nature and therefore it is not necessary to come to know Jesus Christ in order to be saved. However, the Bible makes a clear distinction between those who know of God's existence (demon-like faith as in James 2:19) and those who know God through a second birth (John 3:5; 17:3). According to the Bible, it is not enough to know about God, you must come to know God personally. Romans 1:21 is clear that the darkness that came did not come as a result of what was done but because of what was not done – they refused to give God honor and thanks which led them into darkness. Paul's arguments in Romans 1:22-24 is that the knowledge of God that they do possess is not enough to save them, but it is enough to condemn them because of their lack of response. The Apostle Paul is teaching that these people have not lived up to the light God has given them. Because they did not respond to the light God gave them, they slid even further away from God. Light rejected brings darkness and all kind of sinful behavior and false beliefs (Romans 1:24-32). People can be very sincere in their religion, but sincerely wrong because they have believed a lie (Romans 1:24).

When The Light God Gives Is Received Light Increases

If a person will respond to the light God has given him, then God will give him more light. Romans 1:17 tells me that, **"the righteousness of God is revealed"** which will further lead one from, **"faith to faith."** A person comes to believe in the gospel when he goes step by step from **"faith to faith."** If a person will respond to the light God has given him, then God will give him more light. And when one uses that light, God will give him more light as he goes from **"faith to faith"** – and ultimately God will give him the glorious gospel of Jesus Christ. You see, all men have knowledge of God, but to be saved you have to have a knowledge of Jesus (John 3:36). However, if a person is not interested in *the fact* of God, then God has no obligation to reveal *the way* of God. But when a person is interested in the fact of God as seen in creation and conscience, then God Himself will give that person more light.

This can be illustrated by the life of the Ethiopian Eunuch who was lost but open, so God guided him to a copy of the scroll of Isaiah and a preacher to explain it to him (Acts 8:26-37). Likewise, in Acts 10, Cornelius, a heathen Gentile, did not turn to idols like so many of his contemporaries. He did not embrace the gods of Rome but he responded to the light he had and the one true God gave him more light. He had not heard the gospel—and yet he responded to the light he had and so the Jews describe him as, **"a devout man and one who feared God. . .and gave many alms"** to the poor and **"prayed to God"** (Acts 10:2). Clearly he embraced God's existence enough to fear Him, yet he did not know Jesus Christ and so the Bible describes him as not yet being saved (Acts 11:14). But due to his response to the light, God gave him a vision to go to Joppa, while at the same time in another city God gives Peter a vision to speak to him about Jesus Christ. God gives more light to those who respond to the light they have because God will always meet the responsive searching heart.

By nature, none of us seek God (Romans 3:11), but the Spirit of God will "spring a leak" in your natural heart and give you light—but you must choose to respond (John 12:35-43). A person may be in the depths of the jungle where there is no gospel witness but if he responds to the light he has, God gives more light. But if a person will not respond to the most general of all revelation in creation and conscience, then what would make us think that he will respond to the specific revelation of the gospel? Some people never hear about Jesus Christ for the simple reason they have not responded to the light God has given them. God tells us in Matthew 7:6 that there is a time when we as Christians should withhold 'the gospel pearl' because of a disdain for truth. If God calls us to respond to some people in this manner then you can expect that God practices what He preaches.

All People Have Enough Light To Hold Them Accountable To Christ

The Bible teaches that an individual does not go to Hell for having never responded to a Savior in who he has never heard about, but rather goes to Hell for having rejected the plain truth God has given him. It is a factually true statement that people are judged based on the light they have, and since all have differing amounts of light—there will be differing degrees of retribution. Certainly, the judgment of God in Hell is a terrible thing for anyone who goes—but it will be more worse for some people than for others. Some people have more light and more revelation, not because they necessarily sought it but because of where God sovereignly allowed them to be born. Someone in America will have greater accountability and therefore greater judgment than someone who lives in a country were the gospel witness is not as extensive (Luke 12:47-48).

In Luke 12:47-48, the Lord Jesus uses an illustration from his day as to how masters might deal with their slaves to drive home a spiritual truth about eternal retribution. We must not conclude that because one slave received less of a flogging that Hell is not eternal for some, any more than we should think that the slave who received a longer and more severe flogging had his punishment come to an end. Letting Scripture interpret Scripture, the eternality of Hell is clear, but the degrees of punishment in Hell may somehow differ under God's perfect judicial system. Unmistakably, those who have more light experience a greater judgment as seen in Christ's exhortation to the non-repenting cities of Chorazin, Bethsaida, and Capernaum—as being more accountable—than the cities of Sodom and Gomorrah (Matthew 11:20-24). Those who did not respond will have a more sever judgment than the vile people of Sodom who lived against God in sodomy and adultery. Some individuals are storing up greater wrath for the Day of Judgment because of the greater light they have received and rejected (Romans 2:5-6). The unbeliever can question the justice of God concerning the unevanglized, but the state of those who have heard is very clear (John 3:36; Romans 10:13-15). In one sense, it would be better for an individual to have never heard the gospel than to have heard it and then done nothing with it.

IV. OUR RESPONSE TO THE UNEVANGELIZED

The Bible Is Clear That The Untold Billion Are Lost

The untold billions who die lost—not lost for having rejected a Savior in whom they never heard—but for suppressing the light they have by not responding. All of the false premises on how God will deal with the unevanglized are based on both a wrong view of God and a wrong view of man. The average non-Christian has the tendency to make God a little less "holy and righteous" than He really is. The average Christian has the tendency to make man a little more "sincere and searching" than he really is thereby making him a little less "sinful and unrighteous" than he really is. The error of bringing God down or lifting man up are shattered by Scripture and will only lead to false conclusions on the unevangelized. The unevangelized billions are truly lost and God is truly just (Genesis 18:25 cf. Psalm 89:14). Since there is salvation in no one else (John 14:6; Acts 4:12), and since God desires all people to be saved (Luke 19:10; 1 Timothy 2:5; 2 Peter 3:9), it is reasonable to assume that if a person wants to know the truth—that God is ready to reveal it. But as we have seen, some people will never hear the gospel because they do not want to hear the gospel. If they will not respond to the most general of all revelation God has given them, God is not obligated to give them additional revelation. And so a man is not condemned to Hell for not believing in a Savior whom he has never heard, but for not believing in the revelation God has given him.

The Bible Is Clear That We Are Commissioned To Reach Them

The fact that the untold billions are lost and the reality that God is sovereign in salvation, does not change our responsibility to tell them. We are to evangelize the lost because God commands every child of God to evangelize the entire world (Matthew 28:18-20; Mark 16:15). We must never forget that God is sovereign in the salvation of souls for it is God who saves. It is God who brings men and women under the hearing of the gospel, and in turn, to faith in Christ. But neither must we forget that it is God who imparts His vision to His people of a lost and dying world to take them the gospel—the greatest news anyone can ever hear!

NOTES

NOTES

ABOUT THE AUTHOR

Dr. Carl Broggi is the senior pastor of Community Bible Church in Beaufort, South Carolina, where he has served for twenty-seven years. He holds degrees from Dallas Theological Seminary (Th.M) and Southwestern Baptist Theological Seminary (D.Min). He and his wife Audrey have five children and twelve grandchildren. You can listen to his sermons and follow his ministry through his teaching ministry, Search the Scriptures (**searchthescriptures.org**).

Made in the USA
Columbia, SC
04 November 2024

45267866R00015